VINCENT VAN GOGH COLORING BOOK

1. Self-Portrait -1887

3. Irises -1890

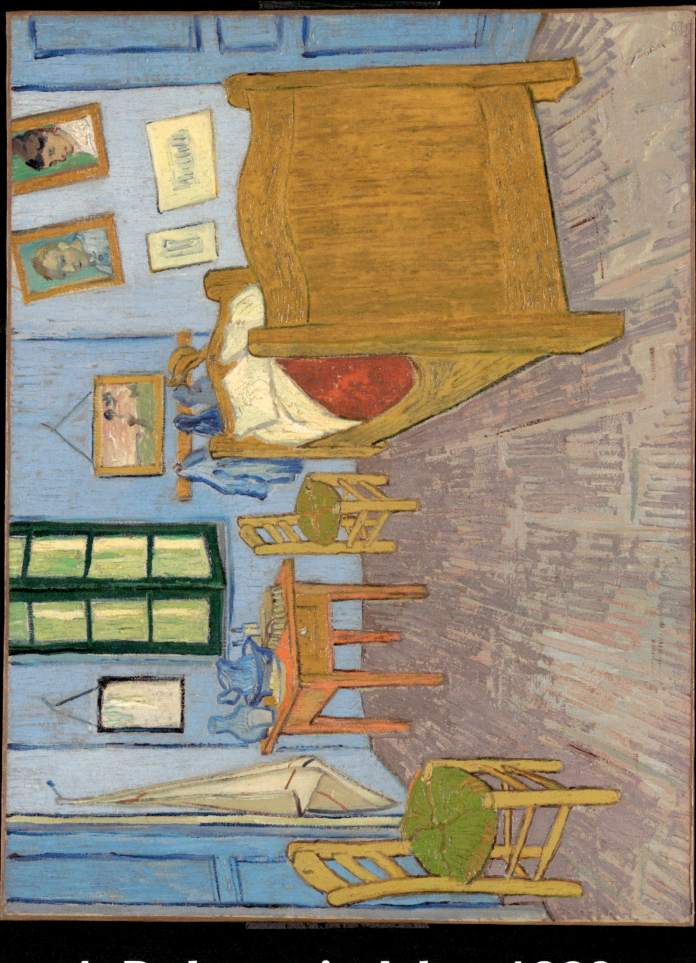

4. Bedroom in Arles -1889

5. Starry Night -1889

6. Portrait of Joseph Roulin -1889

8. Girl in white -1890

9. The night café -1888

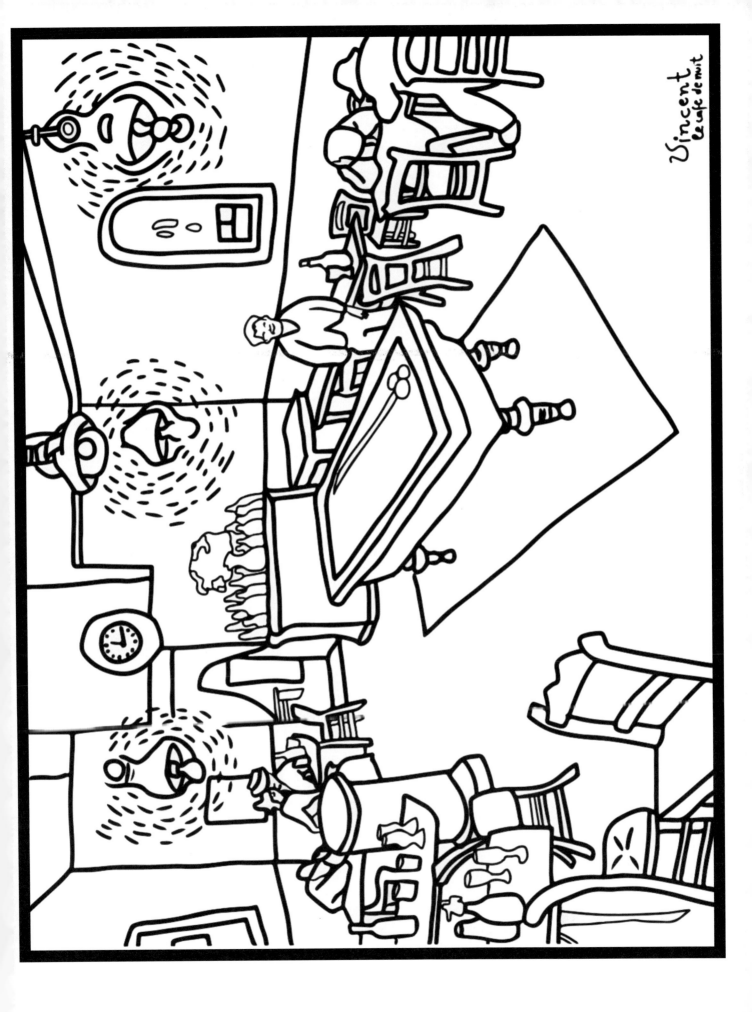

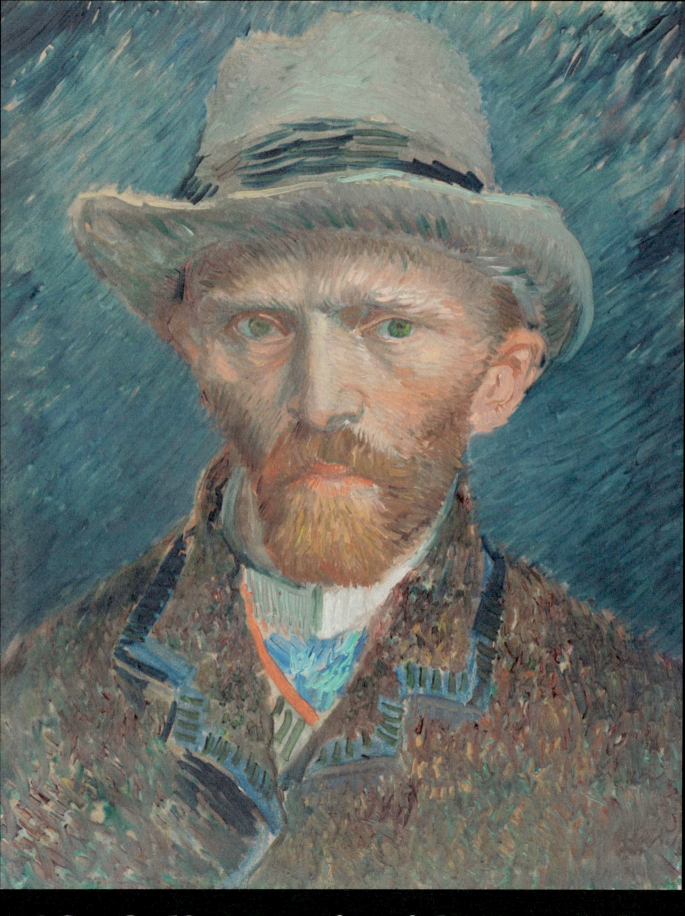

10. Self-portrait with grey felt hat -1886-87

**11.Wheat field
with cypresses - 1889**

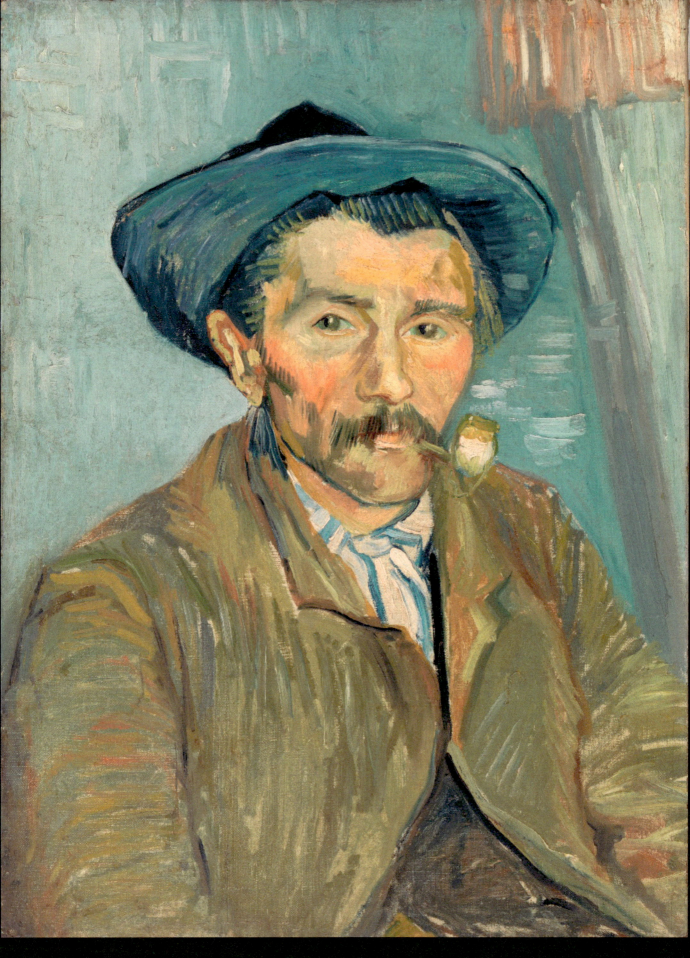

12. Man smoking -1888

13. La mousme sitting-1888

14. Apples -1887-1888

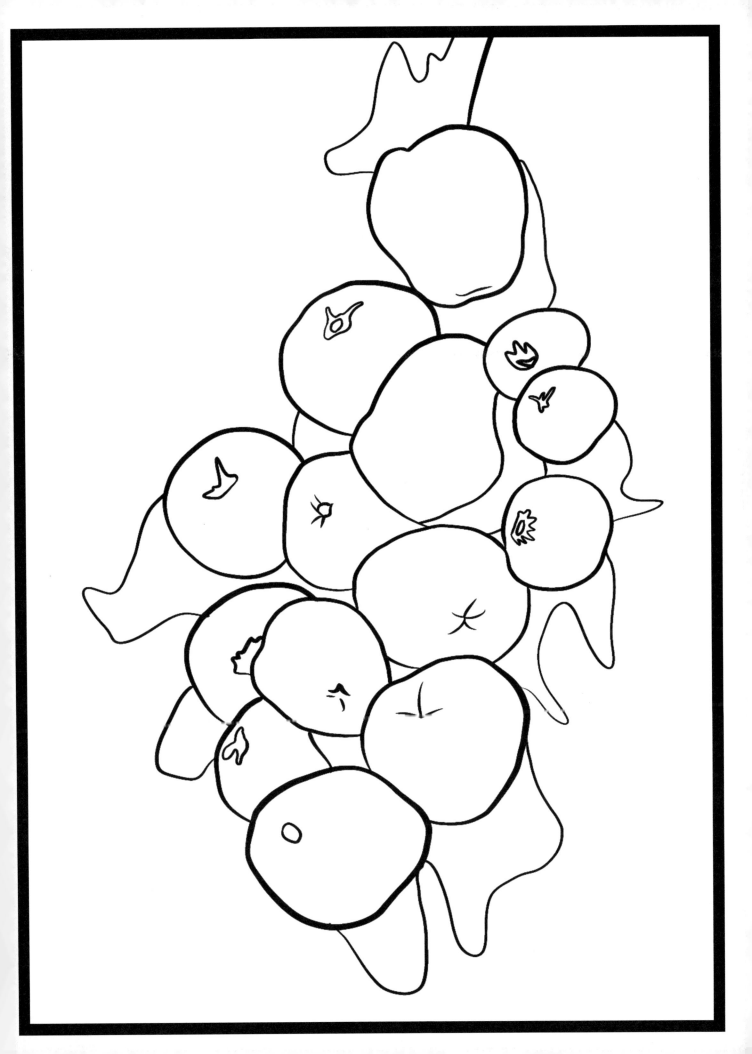

15. La berceuse -1889

16. Landscape with house and Ploughman -1889

17. Self-portrait with grey felt hat -1887

18. Vase with Fifteen Sunflowers-1889

19. Self-Portrait with a Bandaged Ear -1889

20. Sorrowing old man at eternities -1890

21. Starry night over the Rhone -1888

22. The church at Auverse-1889

23. Two cut sunflowers

24. Van Gogh's chair -1888

25. Portrait of the artist's mother

26. Noon rest from work

27. Portrait of Alexander Reid

28. Still life with quinces

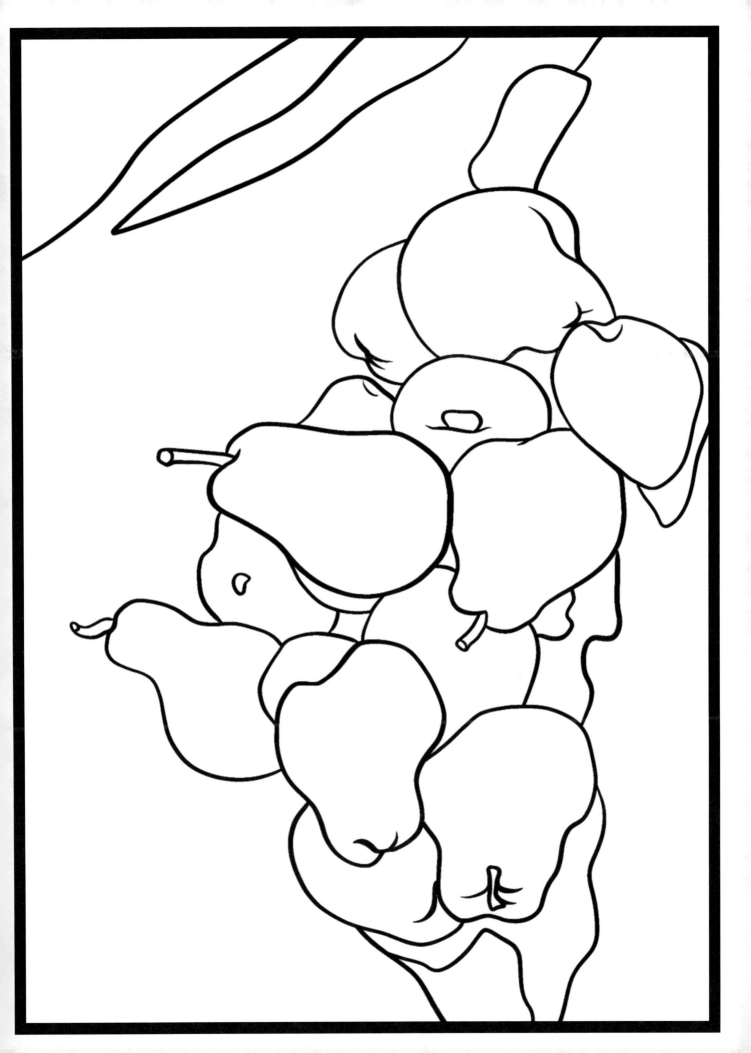

29. Portrait of Madame Ginoux

30. Portrait of Theo Van Gogh

31. Still life detail bottle and

32. An Old Woman of Arles

33. The Mulberry Tree

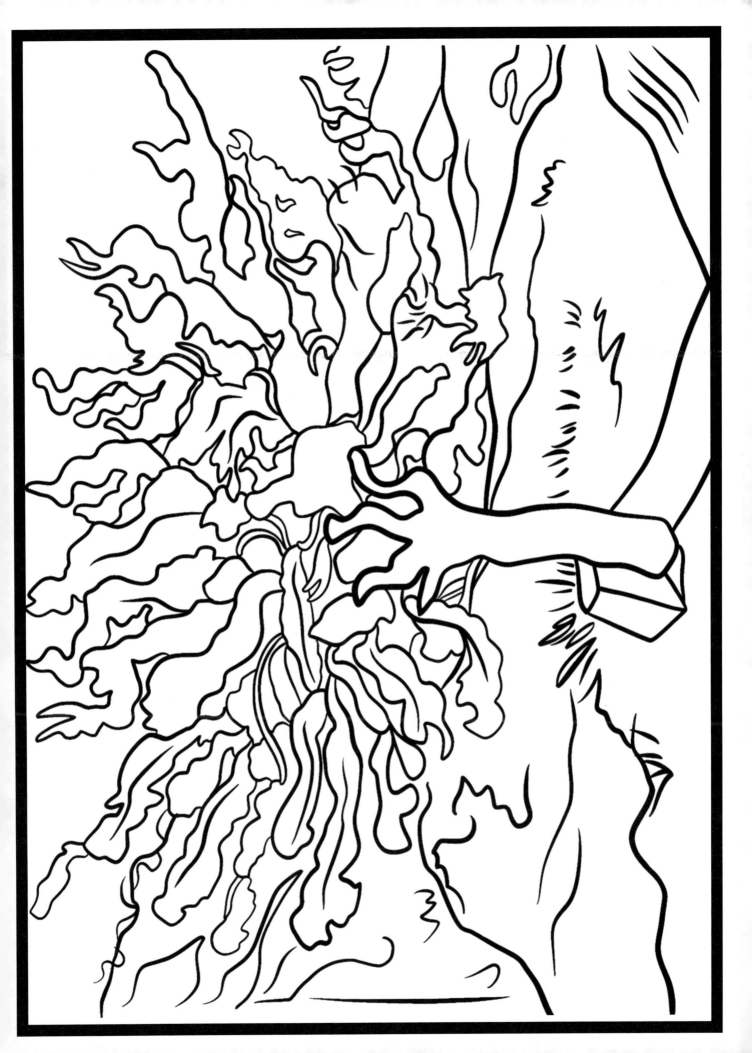

34. Les Alyscamps

35. Giant peacock moth

36. The Gardener

Tag us on Instagram!
@Blackpaper_publishing